Travis I. Sivart

27 Thoughts About Streaming on Twitch

Travis I. Sivart

Travis I. Sivart

27 Thoughts About Streaming on Twitch
27 Thoughts on Social DIY Series, Book 4

Copyright © 2019 Travis I. Sivart

Cover Design by Travis I. Sivart
Edited by Tara Moeller

ISBN: 978-1-954214-41-5

Talk of the Tavern Publishing Group

Travis I. Sivart

Enjoying what you're reading?
Want some more for free?

Go to TravisSivart.com/work

Travis I. Sivart

Dedication

This book is dedicated to all the great people who helped me gain the knowledge about streaming I have. This encompasses the huge audience of Talk of the Tavern, the cast and crew of that same show; Ed, Kevin, Elizabeth, Chris, and Andrea. Especially Andrea, who puts up with all my crazy ideas that include me hogging all the bandwidth.

A special thanks to Jamin and Jewel Skipper for their kind and generous purchase of the image that became the book cover. There's reasons that these two were my first VIPs on Twitch.

A few streamers stand out above the rest though, and a special thanks goes out to Metricula who helped me get started, RWMech who helped with stage two of things, TalkingTowhee who was a constant friend in streaming, and RichieMuenster for all the help with the awesome graphics, overlays, and widgets. Take a few moments to check out their streams on twitch.tv. Oh, and I guess you could drop by my channel and visit me as well. Find me at twitch.tv/TravisTavernSociety

Travis I. Sivart

Contents

27 Thoughts About Streaming on Twitch

27 Thoughts About Streaming on Twitch

Introduction

This is not a complete guide, how to, DIY, or instruction manual for streaming on Twitch.tv. This is a primer, and it should allow you a broad spectrum view of the website that has changed how reality TV works in this modern age of instant gratification, overnight successes, internet famous celebs, and social gaming.

I've been live streaming since March 2017, but have been doing my show – Talk of the Tavern - since 2007. First as a podcast, then in 2012 I switched to live internet radio, and now to live video streaming on Twitch. I've been doing street theatre and interacting with the public as such since 1990, and went to broadcasting school in 2003. Since I published my first book in 2013, I've been a guest at dozens of conventions, and have done numerous live broadcasts.

The point of all that is; I know a bit about presentation and interacting with the public in an entertainment role.

This book will give less technical details (though I touch on a few) and more information regarding best practices in other areas. If you need help setting up stream keys, servers, what computer system is best, the preeminent cameras, good microphones, and other such gear then I recommend you go pull up some YouTube videos. There's a wealth of information, opinion, and experience available at a few keystrokes and/or clicks of your mouse, and they can cover those things with more authority than I ever will be able to.

Keep in mind that technology, software, and Twitch itself is constantly changing, tweaking, growing, adding, and deleting features. What is in this book (written in July 2019) may be out of date in a few weeks, and almost definitely will be less accurate as time marches on.

A few quick things about hardware. You don't need a lot to stream. An X-Box, a PS4, or a cell phone is enough to get started. But to get a lot of the bells and whistles, like overlays, cool text features, emotes, etc., you'll need a computer, a webcam, and a microphone (a gaming headset is fine for this).

The better the equipment, the higher the quality your stream will be, but you can start out simple. I did.

The last thing I want to say in this introduction is that you should always be yourself. You can have your public persona, but always be you also. People can only fake it for so long in the long run. But by being yourself, you can maintain that public persona.

Something that always goes with being yourself is to have fun. You might have decided to stream to make money, get famous, impress someone, or because your dog whispered it to you while your ravioli smiled up at you with its cheesy goodness…but whatever reason, you've decided to do this, remember to have fun. People would rather watch someone awkward who's having fun, than a professional being miserable. That's a truth that you can bank on.

27 Thoughts About Streaming on Twitch

27 Thoughts About Streaming on Twitch

1. Study What You Like

Whether you just discovered Twitch.tv when you picked up this book, or if you've been on it for years, study the channels you enjoy watching.

Take the time to watch streams, notice how the viewers interact, what the layout of the screen is, how the streamer holds themselves, what they say, and how they interact.

If you stay true to yourself you'll create a channel and a stream that reflects the things that you like. You can't do that if you haven't explored what you like.

Take notes, also. When you're watching other streams, write down what you like. What makes you comment, what makes you decide to click on THAT particular stream again and again, and chances are that others will click on your stream for similar reasons.

I speak from experience when I give this advice. I had an established show and converted from internet radio to live video streaming. When I first started my channel, it was bleak, and I set things up that made sense for voice interaction, but not for video. If I had taken more time to explore others already doing what I wanted to do, I could have avoided a steep learning curve.

Travis I. Sivart

2. Being a Viewer

Knowing how to be a good viewer is essential. Knowing how to interact is one thing, but being anxious or afraid to interact is much more common. Understanding that many people are nervous about taking up too much of your attention or time, and because of that they don't chat at all, is very important.

Try to put yourself in their place, remembering the first time you chatted (or if you're my age, then the first time you posted on a blog, social media post, or MUD). Making your viewers comfortable is often learned by realizing how other streamers have put you at ease when you were new.

Was it them greeting you that made you chat? Was it them being passionate about what they were streaming? Was it me raising my glass, toasting some silly thing and laughing that made you type in my channel for the first time? Remember what you felt like, and that empathy will help you win new viewers that come back again and again.

Nothing is worse than a bad houseguest, and the same goes for a viewer that doesn't know how to behave. We all get trolls—my troll rule being: If you're going to be a troll (or an asshole) then at least be an entertaining one—but understanding why they do it is another thing altogether.

Many folks troll because they have other issues at home, school, or work; and the anonymity of the internet makes them feel empowered to bully others. Don't let these people ruin your chat. Bond with them, or kick them. A good troll can be a powerful tool in entertainment, a bad troll can sour a whole crowd.

Travis I. Sivart

3. Software

Twitch.tv can be self-contained, but most folks use software like OBS (Open Broadcaster Software) that allows you to add all kinds of bells and whistles to your stream.

Counters, tip jars, moderator bots, chat timers (things that post certain information at certain points in your stream), multiple cameras, display captures, game captures, and more are all available.

Services like Nightbot, Moobot, StreamElements, StreamLabs, Kappamon (cute critter that interacts with specific commands), and dozens of others are online resources to add all these cool things to your stream.

Keep in mind that they can be a drain on your bandwidth, but with a reasonable internet service and a machine that is mostly up to current specs that will almost never be an issue.

This is one of those things that I recommend haunting YouTube for an afternoon, or a couple days, and see what each offers. Almost anything you see done can be duplicated with just a little effort.

Travis I. Sivart

4. Overlays & Screen Setup

This is expanding on the previous entry in this book. You can have just you on camera, but that is rather plain, and most people will want more than that sooner rather than later.

Some of these are available in services such as StreamLabs and StreamElements as already put together and assembled widgets or overlays. It's just a matter of entering a browser source into OBS or whatever you use.

It might be a game overlay, or just a theme, but it pulls your look together and makes it cohesive and pleasing to the eye.

It also works well with branding your channel, allowing you to create your own overlay and screen layout that is unique to you and your channel. You can piecemeal it together using images from your computer, blended with the widgets available from these online sources.

One thing I really wanted to know how to do—and I couldn't find anything online on how to do it, and no streamer would share this secret—is how to make multiple cameras appear with a cool image over it. Spoiler: you need a digital art program. It's called an overlay. It's as simple as creating a png with a cutout in it that you've deleted and replaced with an invisible background. If that doesn't make sense, turn back to ol' reliable, YouTube.

Travis I. Sivart

5. Below the Screen

When streaming from your computer you'll see a space below the video player on your Twitch channel. This is where you put all the other things.

It's commonly used for social media, tips, links to websites, listing your stream rules, or just letting folks know a little about you and your stream. This is a very important thing. Oh, and don't use too many words, people glaze over. They came to Twitch for video, not reading. Keep it simple.

To add something simply click on the slider that has the words "Edit Panels" to its right. Once you've done that you will have a box with a huge plus sign in it. When you click on that you'll (at the time this book was written) have the choice of "Add a Text or Image Panel" and "Extension Panel".

If you add text or an image—and I highly recommend you add an image for each box, because people react better to pictures than words by themselves—consider adding a link wherever you can. There is a highlighted word within the box that also can show you how use their "Markdown" language (no HTML at the time I wrote this book).

Using matching images, at least themed ones, helps you build your brand. You can make these yourself or have someone else do it (fiverr.com has many folks who will do this, and your emotes, for reasonable prices). If you're adding social media links, you can use standard images/icons for whatever social media you will be linking. People recognize them immediately.

Travis I. Sivart

6. Dashboard: Categories & Tags

Before going live you should at least adjust the category to match the content you'll be streaming. The tags are just a bonus that allows your content type to be further refined, and many people skip them altogether.

I recommend researching categories and see which has more traffic. For example; there is a tabletop role-playing game category and a Dungeons and Dragons category, and the Dungeons and Dragons one always has more viewers. So when I stream D&D, I don't use the first option because it attracts less traffic.

All this is done from the "Creator Dashboard", which you can get to by clicking your channel icon in the upper right to get the drop list, then choose the dashboard from that list.

The dashboard has many helpful tools, some of which I'll cover later, but some are worth pointing out now. I tend to keep the dashboard up whenever I'm streaming so I can see stats, change the title or category as I change what I'm doing mid-stream, or set up a raid at the end of the stream (more on that later).

The dashboard also can show you your stream health, your actual streaming video, place markers so you can find a specific segment later, or control your extensions (which can also be done from the "Extensions" page found on the list to the left of the dashboard).

Travis I. Sivart

7. Choosing Your Content

Here's where we start getting into the meat and potatoes of things. Some folks always stream the same thing and others are variety streamers who stream different things depending on their mood, the day, or the alignment of the stars.

Deciding your content can shape and influence everything about your channel. Streaming the same video game can guarantee you a consistent viewer base because they always know what to expect every time they log in. Variety streaming may draw from a larger viewer base, but it can lead to smaller viewer count because many people don't want a random show every time they stop in.

I'm a variety streamer—streaming a talk show, video games, tabletop role-playing games, writing, and more—and often folks pop in to see what I'm streaming then head off if it isn't what they're in the mood for at that moment. Whereas Ninja, the largest and most popular streamer on Twitch, is almost always playing a shooter video game. People know what to expect, and go to his channel for that content.

Whatever you choose to stream, make sure you have fun with it and are passionate. Those two things attract, and keep, the most people in your channel.

Travis I. Sivart

8. Consistency

People go to a steakhouse for steak, a seafood place for seafood, and a Italian place for pasta. They go to see a comedy to laugh, a horror movie to be scared, and a romantic movie to feel emotions. If you switched it up, and offered something they didn't expect, it'll usually confuse them, and possibly even upset them enough that they don't return.

The same goes for your stream. Keep the tone similar enough, even if you're switching your content, that people know what to expect. Is it a laid-back, chill atmosphere or do you scream obscenities at the game you're playing? Do you have music going and have high energy, or is it usually you quietly doing crafts. Keep enough similarity in your personality and delivery that folks know what to expect out of you.

I will cover schedule in a bit, but you also need consistency in that.

Travis I. Sivart

9. Style

This is a broad spectrum thing, ranging from what you wear, the overall look and feel of your channel, to your personality and attitude.

The first thing most people notice is what their eyes see. This means the overlay of your channel, followed by your personal appearance—if you have a camera, and I highly recommend you do because people connect better with someone they can see—and after that it is your voice, your content, and the garnishes (such as what's below the screen, your emotes, etc.).

Bringing your style together is something that gives you that finished look. It doesn't have to be fancy, it just has to be you. If you're a metalhead, then wear the concert t-shirts and have a bass guitar displayed behind you; if you're a crafter, wear comfy clothes and have a shelf of supplies behind you, etc. I have a relaxed, pub-like atmosphere, so I often wear funny t-shirts, Hawaiian shirts, retro bowling shirts, and have a pipe collection in the background above a mobile bar.

Have your overlay and bottom material match also, or at least match it to your content. So many people do this, and it's like walking into a themed restaurant or store for the mind.

Lastly is your tone, match it to what you do. Not that a metalhead can't be mellow…ever met a bass player?

Travis I. Sivart

10. Confidence

Confidence is key, but leave the ego and arrogance behind.

People come to your channel to see you and what you do. You don't have to be the ultimate authority on what you stream, but own it. Don't let your content scare you. Even if you're doing something that you've never done before (new video game, Twitch Sings, making chainmail, etc.) own that you're a newb at it, and be comfortable with that fact.

Every day streaming is like a job interview; you need to go in like you know what you're doing, even if what you're doing is learning something new. That isn't to say you should act like you're a master of something you've never done, instead you be the master of learning how to do something new.

Arrogance, ego, and the bullying that's implied by either of these are always a turn off. Be encouraging of others when they relate to what you're doing or show appreciation for you and your stream.

Many people have the rule on their stream, "Don't be a Dick", also known as the Wil Wheaton's Rule. It's a good general rule, whether you're the streamer or a viewer.

Travis I. Sivart

11. Your Voice

Most people, even those that talk a lot, don't like the sound of their own voice. But it's your voice, and anyone stopping by your stream are most likely to experience it at some point. This is a part of your charm.

Whether it's deep and resonating, whiney and nasally, sounds like a young child, or just bland in your opinion…others come back to listen to your voice.

We've had some great voices in my generation— Morgan Freeman, Sam Elliot, Eartha Kitt, Stephen Fry, Laurence Fishburne, Alan Rickman, James Earl Jones, Casey Kasem, etc.—but think of your morning show radio hosts. Many of those have less than perfect voices, but thousands of people tune in every day to listen to them.

Your voice is your audio signature, and people recognize it. It doesn't matter if you think it's perfect, what matters is that it's unique to you. That's a bigger and better thing than being anything else.

Think about John Leguizamo, Fran Drescher, Pee-wee Herman, John Waters, Lisa Lampenelli, Chris Rock, and others who don't have the most delightful voice, but we all know them.

Your voice is fine, be proud that it sounds like you in all your glory, and not like anyone else.

Travis I. Sivart

12. Branding (& Emotes)

Branding, according to Dictionary.com means "the promotion of a particular product or company by means of advertising and distinctive design."

Branding is an important thing, it creates a memorable image in the minds of those who see your stream. This can be as simple as coordinating the colors, or as complex as making everything bunny themed.

Think of the "Golden Arches" and McDonalds comes to mind. Or the circle with the red, white, and blue wave in it, and you think of Pepsi. This is brand recognition, and a lot of Twitch streamers are on this bandwagon.

It's a great way to unify your stream and make it instantly recognizable when people see your social media, or anything else you have.

The emotes you can get once you're a Twitch affiliate, and later as a Twitch partner, can be used to further this. Whether it's the art style—such as chibi style, words, or even bar themed like my brand—or matching it to your stream theme, this is the way to make people comfortable with something they recognize and expect.

Travis I. Sivart

13. Your Background

When you're setting up your camera for your stream you should always consider what else people see. The things behind you can set an impression that supports what you do, or it can set an impression that negatively effects those watching.

If you have a geeky or nerdy stream, a wall of comics or character plushies behind you enhances your image. But a pile of dirty laundry and an unmade bed can give you the feel of a messy or even a dirty person.

A green screen allows you to choose any backdrop you like, and is a wonderful way to blend other elements into your stream.

Travis I. Sivart

14. Schedule

This throws back to consistency and treating your stream like a business. Many small businesses fail because they don't keep regular hours. This can be the same for streamers. You don't have to stream all day, or every day, but do choose a schedule that people can rely on.

Choose a day and time, or more than one if you can, and stick to it. People love schedules and knowing when they can find your stream.

I started with one day a week, and even now that I stream almost every day, that Monday time slot at 8 PM Eastern is the one where I see the largest attendance.

Travis I. Sivart

15. What NOT to Stream

This is a tricky thing, because human nature makes us sometimes stream content that no one really cares to see. Three things immediately comes to mind.

First is, don't stream whining. We all have bad days, and things happen in our lives that are frustrating, upsetting, or somehow make us less than happy. It's ok to mention these things, as it can create a personal connection to your viewers and make you more approachable, flawed, relatable, and even likeable. But it isn't ok to do a whole stream to complain about that thing.

Keep your complaining to a minimum, or if you must do it, make it a relatable rant that others can interact with on some level. Bonding and commiserating is different than just crying about something.

Second, try to avoid streams where you spend the whole stream adjusting your interface and overlay, (something I'm guilty of). People like the mystique and illusion of the finished product, and though an occasional adjustment is bound to be necessary, try not to shatter that by spending hours tweaking your stream on air.

Third, don't stream everyday tasks, such as cleaning your room. I've seen a streamer get around this by labeling their stream as 'virtual cleaning simulation' and they kept it entertaining, but that isn't an easy thing to do.

Choosing to do a Marie Kondo style thing, or a cooking stream, or showing how a particular mundane thing can be done with flair can be entertaining, but just trimming your toenails is not.

Travis I. Sivart

16. Building a Community

Start small. One person is how every single community starts, and you are that one person. When the first viewer joins you, making them feel welcome without appearing desperate is a fine line.

Be inclusive. Welcome everyone. If you're streaming a game and the person in your chat says they have never played the game, it's the perfect time to show your passion for the game. Be excited and include your viewers in what you're doing, and that will make them come back again.

Be supportive. When someone pops in and tells you about when they did the same thing you are currently doing, let them know that you think that is great! They admire you and want your approval and support, they want to connect with you over this common interest, and are giving you the chance to make them want to come back.

Offer something unique. There's a lot of streamers out there offering the same type as stream as you. You're the one thing that others cannot duplicate. You, your personality, and your view on the activity you are partaking of; use that to make folks know you're offering something no one else on Twitch is offering.

People watch Twitch to socialize. They come to your stream to be able to talk about something they like, or even love. Interact with them about it, and let them help you create the content you need for your stream.

Travis I. Sivart

17. Talking (to Viewers)

As I just mentioned, people come to Twitch to socialize, and talking is an essential part of that.

Even when you have no viewers, keep a steady stream of consciousness going (there are exceptions to this, like coworking streams). Banter with yourself. Narrate your current activity. Whatever it takes, just keep talking.

People pop in and out of streams constantly, looking for one person or thing that will capture their attention and make them stick around. If you're talking when they check out your channel, they're more likely to interact, and stay on your channel.

Nothing makes me flick to the next stream quicker than seeing someone who appears to be frozen except for the occasional sound of a mouse click. Even if they have a game on most of the screen; I can play the same game and see the same thing. But if they're talking, then I have something unique and different that I can't find anywhere else.

When someone types something in chat, try acknowledging them as soon as you can, even if it's to say, 'Hold on just a minute while I finish this thing...' to let them know that you value them being there. They'll understand if you're in the middle of an intense fight, or completing a complex maneuver in whatever creative thing you're working on.

On a related note, keep in mind some folks just want to lurk and watch. Don't force someone to chat if they don't want to, even if they were chatty last time they popped in.

Travis I. Sivart

18. Favoritism to Viewers

Once your community begins to grow, you'll have regulars. Some people will be the ones you always talk to, others will subscribe and never say a thing, and so on. It's okay to play favorites, but never to the point where you ignore others.

The people you talk with will help draw in new viewers. As you gain regulars you'll relegate some of them to moderators, VIPs (more about that later), and so on.

Also, some viewers require more attention than others, and some less, but almost all of them require some attention. A good rule of thumb is that if they post in chat, they want at least a hello.

Asking viewers questions makes them feel like part of the stream, and shows they have value to you as a viewer. Don't let any single viewer dominate your stream, if they want all the attention then they should have their own stream.

I recommend you always acknowledge a new follow, subscription or resub, bits thrown, donation or tip, host, raid, etc. Make them feel appreciated for supporting you and your channel in whatever form.

Travis I. Sivart

19. Rules & Setting Boundaries

On Twitch you can set up rules for chat and they pop whenever someone chats for the first time in your stream. Lots of folks will also insert these rules into the area below the video player.

There are a lot of folks who use the same rules, and most of them are basic social courtesies, such as not being a jerk or spewing hate.

You're not required to have rules, and in my case I used the pop up rules as a chance to remind viewers that my stream is an adult stream.

But, whether you post rules or not, do set boundaries…for your own sake. This is different than rules, though the boundaries you set can be reiterated in your rules.

Decide what you're comfortable with and stick by it. This might be if you allow "back-seat gaming", swearing, flirting, exchange of personal information, or anything else.

Don't feel bad enforcing these rules or boundaries, either. This is your channel, your stream, your house, and you get to make the rules (within the parameters of the Twitch Terms of Service, or ToS).

Give people a warning if they're breaking the rules if you are feeling generous, post the rules if you want, but the bottom line is that you get to decide what behavior is acceptable, and you can time out or even ban anyone, for any reason.

Travis I. Sivart

20. Bringing on Guests

I get a lot of viewers asking to come on my stream with me, as in using their microphone and camera and joining me live and on air. I recommend caution with this practice.

I invite people on for a couple of reasons, but usually because I want to interview them (I do run a talk show format), or because they're a friend and I know we can have a good and interactive conversation together.

No matter the reason I decide to invite them I always explain what's expected of them, which includes; acceptable language and topics, interacting with viewers who post in chat (even if it interrupts our conversation), and the length of their visit on the stream.

I always run a test on their equipment before we go live. Nothing ruins a stream quicker than bad connection or gear. No one wants to suffer through not being able to understand the person on the stream due to technical issues.

Before every stream with more than just myself I do all the things I listed above, from doing a sound and camera check, to going over our topic and time it's expected to last.

Travis I. Sivart

21. Raids & Hosts

When not streaming you have the option of hosting other streamers that are live. You can do this with a command from your own chat box, through your dashboard, or you can set it up to do it automatically.

When you host someone it simulcasts their stream to your channel, allowing your viewers to watch the other stream, with the option for them to go straight to that stream.

Raids are a cool way for you to move all your current viewers at the end of your stream to another streamer's channel. This is often met with excitement and appreciation.

Both these things are a great way to build community, especially if it is reciprocated.

And with that last sentence, let me offer a word of caution; I've raided other channels and lost regular viewers. I've also been mocked when I showed up to a larger stream with only a handful of viewers.

This is why it's important to make sure if you're supporting other people's channels they are doing the same for you. This is a great way to grow, but always just giving is a way to lose more than you gain.

Travis I. Sivart

22. VS&M

VS&M streams, as I like to call them, stands for VIPs, Subscriber, and Moderator streams. These are streams, set up in your dashboard before you go live, that allow only the aforementioned roles to view your stream. The general public get a five-minute free preview, but if they want to see more they'll have to subscribe to your channel or you'll have to assign the role of VIP or moderator to them.

This type of stream leaves many people scratching their heads, and wondering why anyone would want to do a stream where everyone can't view it. I've effectively used it for specialty streams that I want to make private or exclusive for those who have showed extraordinary support, in time spent watching or financial, to my channel.

Doing this has given my viewers the feel of being special, which they are, because of the amazing support they've given my channel. This doesn't mean it would work for everyone and I recommend you use common sense and best judgement before choosing to do this.

I would like to note here that all Twitch ToS still apply, and you cannot do or show anything in a VS&M stream that is against the ToS.

Travis I. Sivart

23. Reruns, Clips, Highlights, & Premieres

These four things are ways to have extra content that isn't a live stream. You, or any viewer, can clip a segment from your live stream by clicking the "clapperboard" (you know, that thing they use in Hollywood when shouting, 'TAKE TWO!") in the lower right of the video player. When you click the icon, it will open a new tab and allow you to choose up to sixty seconds of the previous ninety seconds of the stream to clip out and save. You just need to give it a name.

In your dashboard, you can choose the "Video Broadcast" feature where you can upload a "Premiere", a pre-recorded video, to play at that time. It can also play any saved previously aired videos or highlights (up to 24-hours worth, you can create a playlist) as a "Rerun".

To make a highlight, you can choose the "Video Producer" from the list on the left of the dashboard. Once there it brings you to a list of previous videos. To the right of each one will be a highlight button where it will allow you to trim an episode to the desired length and save it forever!

Travis I. Sivart

24. Making Money

Bits, Tips, Merchandise, and Sponsors, Oh My!

It's possible to make money on Twitch, though I discourage you from going into streaming with that being your only goal.

Once you're a Twitch Affiliate or Partner your viewers will have the ability to subscribe and throw bits. Subscriptions, at the time of the writing of this book, pay $5 to $25, of which the streamer gets half and Twitch gets the other half. Bits can be bought for money, and then "thrown" (as the terminology goes) at streamers. They are worth a penny a bit, but it adds up quickly.

Besides that, you can open a merchandise (merch) store through any of the online stores available and provide the link in the area below the video player.

The last way to make money is to get sponsors, though this is usually reserved for those who have large audiences, and is best researched extensively outside of this book.

Travis I. Sivart

25. Affiliate & Partner

Twitch has streamers, affiliates, and partners. Anyone can be a streamer, but to be an affiliate or partner you need to reach specific benchmarks known as achievements.

At the time of the writing of this book, to be an affiliate you need to reach fifty followers, stream for eight hours in a month, stream on seven different days in a month, and have an average of three viewers over that month.

To be a partner, you need to stream for twenty-five hours in a month, stream on twelve different days in a month, and have an average of seventy-five viewers over that month.

Once you reach these goals, affiliate and partner status allows you to make money via bits and subscriptions, have custom emotes (supplied by you, not Twitch), have loyalty badges (icons for your subscribers), subscriber-only chat or archives, and more.

Travis I. Sivart

26. All Things = Art (or Just Chatting)

Okay, here's where we get into opinion. When choosing a category, it's best to choose the game you're playing. But sometimes you're not streaming a game, but something...different. And if you have no idea what category to choose, you can always choose "Art".

Art is subjective, and you can choose the "Art" category for many things if you can't find any other category that fits. I'm looking at a stream under art called, "A Jar of Peanut Butter" as I write this sentence. Lots of things fall under art, such as knitting, chainmail, kittens playing, writing, explosive fires, and so on.

If that doesn't fit and you are talking as you stream, then consider using "Just Chatting", another catch-all that is useful for so many streams that don't fit into any other category.

Travis I. Sivart

27. Final Thoughts

I want to reiterate a few things from the introduction here...

One, have fun. Having fun and being passionate about what you're doing is worth a thousand cool overlays or the best gear you can buy.

Two, be yourself. Own it and let your inner self come out and play. People can sense someone being fake, and then you're not really one of the cool kids. Instead, you're just a poser and a pretender begging for attention.

Three, though it wasn't mentioned in the introduction but, treat your stream like a business and you'll be better off. Be open to changing, improving, upgrading, and listening to constructive criticism. Never stop learning and growing.

Four, this book is not an all-encompassing tutorial. Go out and research more. This is just basics, and bit of image coaching. Go look into streams, YouTube videos, ask advice, and learn more than can be contained between these covers.

And lastly, come by my stream and say hello. Let me know you read this and how it helped. I'd love to discuss these things and more, and maybe even learn something new from you. You can find me most days doing my thing at twitch.tv/TravisTavernSociety.

Travis I. Sivart

Enjoying what you're reading?
Want some more for free?

Go to TravisSivart.com/work

Travis I. Sivart

About the Author

Travis I. Sivart is a prolific author of Fantasy, Science Fiction, Social DIY, and more. He's created The Traverse Reality, a shared universe that connects his cyberpunk, fantasy, and steampunk worlds, and writes characters who feel real to his readers.

You can sometimes find him live-streaming the writing and editing of his latest project from his home in Central Virginia, surrounded by too many cats.

You can find Travis at www.TravisISivart.com.

Travis I. Sivart

If you enjoyed this book...

Please let others know by reviewing it on Amazon or Goodreads, and let others know your thoughts!

Other books by Travis I. Sivart:

Aetheric Elements: The Rise of a Steampunk Reality

Automatons and airships, bustles and beasts, corsets and curses, dandies and dastardly deeds, all await you as you explore the cultures which evolved into a Steampunk industrial civilization. An anthology of nineteen tales of terror, mystery, and adventure.

Steampunk For Simpletons: A Fun Primer For Folks Who Aren't Sure What Steampunk Is All About

A primer followed by a guided tour through the world of steampunk, from the basics such as where to go and what to do, to the aesthetic of the arts within steampunk.

Journal of a Stranger

The thoughts, ideas, philosophies, and inspirations of a time traveling adventurer. Delving into the psychology of man, life's eternal questions, burning passions, and the quirky pseudo-science of his mind, and more.

The Downfall: Harbinger

The Talisman came again, but this time it didn't leave. The magical emanations of the comet have brought terrors from the bowels of the earth and increased the powers of an insane necromancer. The chaos above brought out others seeking to wrest control of the land. Five people from different walks of life are thrown together by these events with the knowledge that the world as they know it is ending.

27 Thoughts About Streaming on Twitch

Travis I. Sivart

www.ingramcontent.com/pod-product-compliance
Lightning Source LLC
Chambersburg PA
CBHW031230120626
46545CB00003B/1060